A complete guide to raising funds for the environment.

Written
by
Stuart A. Kallen

Published by Abdo & Daughters, 4940 Viking Dr., Suite 622, Edina, Minnesota 55435.

Library bound edition distributed by Rockbottom Books, Pentagon Tower, P.O. Box 36036, Minneapolis, Minnesota 55435.

Edited by Julie Berg

Cover photograph by Vic Orenstein
Interior photographs by Vic Orenstein
Special thanks to the Target Earth™ Kids–Jennie, Libby, Joe, Ted, Kenny & Grace
Artistic Consultant: Patti Marlene Boekhoff

Library of Congress Cataloging-in-Publication data

Kallen, Stuart A., 1955-
     Eco-fairs & Carnivals / written by Stuart A. Kallen.
         p.   cm. -- (Target Earth)
     Includes bibliographical references.
     ISBN 1-56239-205-0
     1. Environmental education--Activity programs--Juvenile literature.
     2. Fund raising--Juvenile literature. I. Title. II. Title: Eco-fairs and carnivals. III. Series.
     GE77.K34   1993
     372.3'57--dc20
                                           93-4156
                                         CIP
                                         AC

 Thanks to the trees from which this recycled paper was first made.

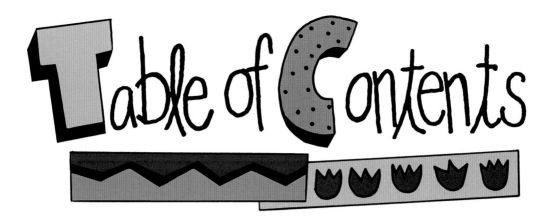

Table of Contents

Chapter 1

An Earth Fair For Funds

Laaay-dees and gentlemen! Step right up to the most beee-dazzling, stuuu-pendous, and inn-c r e d i b l e carnival you've ever seen. We've got great games. We've got frolicking fun. We've got super shows. We've got thrills, chills, and no oil spills. You'll have more fun than a barrel full of birthdays. And we're doing it all for the planet Earth — the greatest show of all.

For Love or Money

In a perfect world, groups that help the environment would have plenty of money to do their work. Volunteers would line up to help. Corporations would donate oodles of money for worthwhile eco-projects. Whether it was for whales or rainforests, the environment would benefit and all would be right with the planet.

But in the real world, it takes lots of money to solve big problems. Environmental groups have to protect animals, lobby politicians, and educate people to stop pollution. All the activities that environmental groups do cost millions of dollars. Most of the groups rely on people to support them. "That's fine," you might say, "but how can I help?" That's where this book comes in.

Eco-Fairs and Carnivals is a book that will tell you how to have Earth-fairs. It will tell you ways that you can make money with the fair and donate it to environmental causes.

You might want to donate the money to a local park. Many small city and local parks could use extra funds for cleaning and fixing-up. That would help the local environment. Or, you could donate the money to a large world-wide organization that might be cleaning up pollution in the Soviet Union or researching plant medicine in the rainforests. You could donate the money to the A B C's of endangered animals, from aardvarks to zebras. The cause is up to you. If you can't decide, there's a list of environmental groups (on page 36) who could put your money to good use.

There are thousands of worthy causes that can use your help. And while you're doing good work for the Earth, you can have lots of fun and learn things.

Gather a Group

Eco-fairs and carnivals use a lot of people power. Unless you have super-human talents, you will need to form a group to help with the carnival. A group of five to thirty people is ideal. It depends on how many people will come to your carnival and how much space you have to put it on.

The best place to find a group of people for your carnival committee is at school. You may want to have an eco-fair as a class project. If not, you may be able to put up fliers on bulletin boards at school asking for volunteers. Other places you can find people to help with your eco-fair:

● Church or temple

● Sports team

● Camp

● Scout troop

● Neighborhood friends

● Chamber of Commerce

● Youth Organization

● The United Way

● Park & Recreation Dept.

Planning Your Eco-Fair

Once you have a group of willing volunteers, you must have several meetings to plan your eco-fair. Here are some basic rules to follow at your meetings.

Step 1 Pick a time when everyone will be able to come to the meetings. After school, Saturday mornings, or week nights are usually good times. It doesn't matter when, as long as most people can attend. Two meetings a week for several weeks should give you plenty of time to plan your eco-fair. At the end of each meeting, you can decide when and where the next one will take place.

Step 2 Pick a chairperson who will keep everything on track and organized. This person should have the skills and the time to work for the eco-fair. If you want to be the chairperson, say so at the first meeting. Vote or get a general agreement as to who it will be.

Step 3 Find an adult who will help. If you are raising money, an adult can help insure that the money is directed where it is supposed to go. A treasurer should be chosen for the group.

Step 4 Decide what group you are going to donate the money to. You may want to pick one cause or you may want to divide the money between several causes. See page 36 for a list of honest and effective environmental groups.

Step 5 Decide when you will have the eco-fair. Again, after school or Saturday afternoons are usually a good time. Be sure to have it far enough in the future to plan it properly. But be sure to have it soon enough so that the group stays interested.

Step 6 Decide where you will have the eco-fair. Wherever you decide, you will need permission to use the space. Make a list of four or five of the best places. After the meeting, the chairperson should try to arrange permission to use those places. Get a written contract if possible. Here are some places you may want to have the eco-fair:

- Courtyard of shopping mall
- Parking lot of local business
- Local park or playground
- Church or temple
- Public library
- Convention center
- School playground
- School gym
- Someone's yard

Step 7 Decide who is going to do each job. Every person has his or her own talents. When you have an eco-fair, everyone can put their best talents to work. At your meeting divide the work into the following committees:

- Food
- Entertainment
- Games and prizes
- Clean-up and recycling director
- Artwork, posters, and promotion
- Coordinator of volunteers
- with adult help - treasury, transportation & sponsors

Step 8 Once you have divided the work into committees, each group may gather separately to organize their part. The following chapters will help each group organize their share of the eco-fair.

You've probably heard the expression, "It takes money to make money." This is also true when it comes to eco-fairs. Your group is going to have to raise "seed" money to get things started. You will need these funds to:

- make or buy prizes for games
- buy art supplies
- buy miscellaneous supplies
- buy food and drinks to sell
- printing costs for posters
- advertising

The easiest way to raise seed money is to ask everyone in the group to make a donation. If you have a group of twenty and everyone donates $10, you will have a good amount of seed money for your eco-fair. Keep a list of the amount everyone donates. After the fair, pay everybody back from the total funds.

If you cannot raise money that way, have a bake sale or ask an adult or business to sponsor your eco-fair. Be sure to give your sponsor credit for their support in your advertising.

Money can be helpful or it can cause problems. To handle money responsibly, you should:

Step 1 Have an adult help manage the money. They can write checks and make sure that the money is spent wisely.

Step 2 Plan how you will spend the money in advance. Decide exactly what prizes, food, and artwork are needed. Go to the store and write down how much everything you need costs. After you are aware of prices, you can pick and chose which items are most necessary.

Step 3 Keep the receipts from everything you buy in a big envelope. Keep a sheet of paper with an inventory of the items bought with their cost listed.

Step 4 Before the fair, make sure you have enough coins and small bills to make change.

Step 5 During the fair, keep a central bank in a safe place. Money can be deposited there, and change can be made. The treasurer should keep track of the money during the fair.

Step 6

After the fair, add up the total funds, pay back all borrowed money, pay any outstanding bills, and send the rest to your favorite environmental cause.

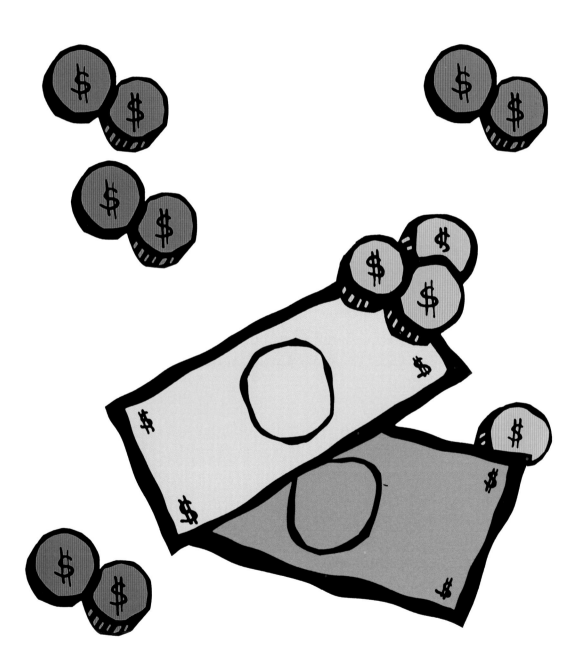

General Rules for Eco-Fairs

With all the fun and games going on at your fair, make sure no mistakes or accidents will happen. If you are going to be responsbile citizens, you must run your carnival in a fair and honest manner. Here are some general rules:

Step 1 Have one or more adults supervise your eco-fair. You might want to have one adult who acts as a "security guard" to make sure everything stays honest and peaceful.

Step 2 If possible, charge a small admission at the gate. This money will help offset other expenses.

Step 3 Keep prices low. Nickles, dimes, and quarters really add up. If you charge too much, people might feel cheated. The idea is to have fun and raise money, not make a fortune.

Step 4 Make sure all the games are honest. Charge enough to cover prizes and make a small profit.

Step 5 Have the eco-fair in a place where bathrooms are available.

Step 6 Make sure there are plenty of places to throw away garbage. Each box should be plainly labeled - glass, aluminum, paper, garbage. That way you can recycle your trash when the fair is over. Many city recycling companies donate containers and arrange for drop-off and pick up.

Chapter 2
Fun Food for Eco-Fairs

If you're having a fair for the environment, you have to sell food that is healthy for people and the planet. Cheeseburgers, hot dogs, and junk food **DO NOT** fit in this category. But you still want foods that are easy to make and serve. There are plenty of cookbooks in the library that contain recipes for food that is healthy and easy to make. Here are a few suggestions for food:

● cookies, muffins, baked goods - try to find recipes that use honey instead of sugar

● bean and cheese tacos and burritos

● Peanut butter and jelly sandwiches on whole wheat bread - if you can find it, you can also use cashew butter, almond butter, or tahini (sesame butter)

● crackers and cheese

● sliced vegetables

● sugar-free fruit juices - orange juice, grape juice, honey-sweetened lemonade

● bottled water

● sugar-free soda

In addition, you will need napkins, paper plates and garbage boxes. You should have four garbage boxes at each food station, each plainly labeled - glass, aluminum, paper, garbage.

IMPORTANT: Some of the food must be prepared before the fair, such as slicing vegetables or making tacos. Make sure that all food is handled in a sanitary manner. This means washing your hands thoroughly, and making the food in a clean kitchen. After the food is prepared, put it in clean, plastic containers and keep refrigerated until the fair. Do not prepare any food that will spoil quickly. It is best to have an adult help with food preparation. If you don't feel that you can prepare food properly, don't make any. Your eco-fair will work without it.

Chapter 3
Art and Promotion for Eco-Fairs

Back in the old days, when the carnival came to town, everybody knew it was coming weeks before it arrived. That's because the carnival advertised and promoted itself. They did this through posters, newspaper stories, radio ads, and in later years, television ads. By the time the carnival arrived, the excitement had been building for weeks. You can advertise your eco-fair in the same manner. Good promotion will draw larger crowds and help make your eco-fair a success.

Two kinds of people are needed for good promotion; artists - people who can draw, pain, and letter; and writers - people who can write well, mail letters, and make effective phone calls.

Artists Jobs Include:

● Drawing and lettering posters

● Making banners

● Painting, silkscreening, or tie-dying T-shirts to sell at the fair

● Decorating the fairground with streamers and crepe paper

● Decorating booths for games (see chapter 5—page 21)

● Helping the entertainment committee with stage sets, costumes, and posters (see chapter 4—page 19)

In addition, artists may want to buy some face paint and run a fair booth painting people's faces. Artists can also sell their arts and crafts at fair booths or donate them for game prizes.

Writers Jobs Include:

● writing copy for posters

● writing short plays and skits for shows (see chapter 4—page 19)

● writing "promo" announcements for radio, TV, and newspapers

● contacting radio, TV, and newspapers to promote the eco-fair

● contacting the environmental organizations you have chosen to help

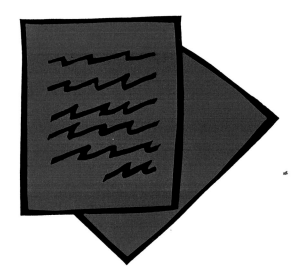

Promotion for Your Eco-Fair

Radio stations, television stations, and newspapers like to run "community news" stories and might be happy to make announcements about your eco-fair. Beside the major stations and newspapers, don't forget to contact small, community newspapers, local access channels on cable TV, and college radio stations.

When writing copy for posters and announcements, make sure to state clearly **why, what, where,** and **when** you are having the eco-fair. Be sure to state which environmental organization will receive the profits. Be sure that all words are spelled correctly.

Contact the organizations for which your fair is raising money. They may be able to provide posters, T-shirts, buttons, and other items that you can sell. They can also provide information and brochures about fund-raising tips and the work they perform.

Posters for Your Eco-Fair

After you have the artwork and copy for your posters, photocopy them on colorful paper. Many photocopy shops are very inexpensive. They may even donate their services if asked.

Here are some places to put up posters:

● Ask local businesses to put them in their store windows.

● Put them up on bulletin boards in schools, grocery stores, church or temple.

● Mail them to radio, TV stations, and newspapers.

● Make sure you do not litter with the posters. After the carnival, go back, collect the posters, recycle them, use them for scrap paper, or save them for your next carnival.

Chapter 4
Entertainment for Eco-Fairs

What would a fair be without entertainment? And there are so many ways to entertain that almost everybody can get into the act. At the eco-fair, everybody's a star.

Here are some suggestions for entertainment:

● Skits or short plays with environmental themes. See the play in the *Eco-Educator's Guide* titled "Mama Earth and the Rocking R's."

Either write a play or try to find one in the library. If you make one up, you can copy a famous play, TV show, or movie. Just re-write it to have an environmental theme.

● Puppets

You can act out eco-themes using hand-made puppets. Libraries have books with information about puppet theater.

● Parades

Everyone loves a parade. You can make floats and costumes from recycled materials. Make signs and banners advertising your event. Have the parade route end at the fair. That way everyone watching the parade will follow it in. Libraries have books with information about parades and costumes.

● Music and dance

Music for the fair can be anything from single entertainers to the school band. Rap and rock bands are fun but might draw complaints because of the noise level. If there are any dancers in your group, they might want to perform. Musicians can also bring kazoos, shakers, and rhythm instruments for people to play.

● Circus acts

Other entertainment can include juggling, clowns, bicycle and skateboard tricks, pet tricks, and silly human tricks.

● Sports and contests

You can have sporting contests such as jumping rope, sack races, egg and spoon races.

Chapter 5

Games for Eco-Fairs

Games are as much a part of the traditional fairs as cotton candy and ferris wheels. Here's a guide to making carnival games from recycled materials. Have people with artistic talent help construct booths, signs, and decorations for the games.

Recycled Bottle Ring Toss

The game of Ring Toss or "Hoop La" is about as old as the carnival itself.

You will need these items

● One or two liter plastic soda bottles, cleaned and rinsed

● Sturdy string, twine or yarn - colorful yarn is best!

● Glass bottles or jars cleaned and rinsed   ● Tape

● A table, crate, or large cardboard box   ● Paper

● Chalk or a small stick   ● A pen, pencil, or marker

● Scissors or hack saw (ask an adult to help you)

How to Make the Ring Toss:

Step 1
Using the scissors or saw, CAREFULLY cut the plastic bottle into strips about one inch (2.5 centimeters) thick. Recycle the neck and the bottom of the bottle.

Step 2
Wrap the string, twine, or yarn around the plastic rings until they are completely wrapped. This should give the rings enough heft for throwing.

Step 3
On a table, crate, or cardboard box set twelve bottles and jars in three rows of four across. Make sure the rings are big enough to go around the bottles. Small blocks of wood can also be used for this purpose.

Step 4
Draw a chalk line on the ground about five feet (1.5 meters) in front of the table with the bottles. Players have to stand behind that line when tossing the rings. Adjust chalk line and table to make the game challenging but not impossible. If you are playing in the grass, a thin stick about 3 feet (one meter) long can be laid down for a line.

For Prizes:

Step 1
Take one of each prize and put it on a numbered piece of paper where players can see it.

Step 2
Write numbers on bottles that match the prizes.

How to Play the Ring Toss:

Step 1 Each player gets three rings.

Step 2 Players stand behind the chalk line and try to throw rings over bottles or wood blocks on the table.

Step 3 Leaning is allowed, but players must keep both feet on the ground.

Step 4 Player wins the prizes that match the numbers on the bottles.

Bean Bag Toss

This is a fun game for fair-goers who think they have a good pitching arm. Sometimes the game is called "Knock Over The Cans."

You will need these items

● About one pound (.45 kilogram) of dried beans. Medium sized beans such as pinto beans or soy beans are the best. Popcorn works to!

● Strong tape

● Sand or gravel

● Rubber bands

● Clean old socks

● Ten empty soup cans

● A table and a box
   a large box and a smaller box

How to Make the Bean Bag Toss

Step 1 Make sure the soup cans are clean and remove their labels. Cans should be standard size soup cans, about 2 5/8 X 4 inches (about 6.3 X 10.1 centimeters). Do not use aluminum cans.

Step 2 Fill all of the cans with gravel, dirt or sand.

Step 3 Tape the tops of the cans shut and wrap a rubber band around the tape edge to hold it on tight. Make sure the tops are tight and will not leak.

Step 4 Fill the end of a sock with about 1/4 pound (112.8 grams) of beans.

Step 5 Tie the beans tight by knotting the sock. Cut off the remaining cloth. Make four or more beanbags in this manner.

Step 6 Set a smaller box on top of a larger box or table.

Step 7 Stack the soup cans on box as in example.

Step 8 Draw a chalk line on the ground about eight feet (2.5 meters) in front of the table with the cans. Players have to stand behind that line when tossing the bean bags. Adjust chalk line and table to make the game challenging but not impossible. If you are playing in the grass, a thin stick about 3 feet (one meter) long can be laid down for a line.

How to Play the Bean Bag Toss

Step 1 Players throw the bean bags and try to knock over the cans.

Step 2 Paint numbers on cans and added up points for how many cans are knocked over.

Step 3 Prizes may be awarded to those knocking over all the cans or by points.

Bucket Toss

An easy-to-make toss game for fun or prizes.

You will need these items

● Soft balls, tennis balls, or any other kind of medium-sized ball

● Three small buckets, baskets, or large cans

● A sturdy board about 3 feet by 3 feet (1 meter by 1 meter)

● Something to prop up one end of the board

● A hammer and small nails   ● Chalk or a stick   ● A table

How to Make the Bucket Toss

Step 1 Hammer buckets to board as in example.

Step 2 Prop up one end of the board on table as in example.

Step 3 Draw a chalk line on the ground about 6 feet (2 meters) in front of the table with the buckets. Players have to stand behind that line when tossing the balls. Adjust chalk line and table to make the game challenging but not impossible. If you are playing in the grass, a thin stick about 3 feet (one meter) long can be laid down for a line.

How to Play the Bucket Toss

Step 1 Players stand behind the chalk line and throw balls into buckets. This is not as easy as it sounds, because balls bounce out of buckets quite easily.

Step 2 Points are scored by adding the numbers on the baskets where the balls landed.

Step 3 Prizes are awarded by number of points scored.

Plastic Bottle Bowling Alley

This game needs to be played on a smooth surface like a driveway or sidewalk.

You will need these items

- Ten large plastic soda bottles with tops

- A soccer ball, soft ball, or basketball

- Chalk

- Dirt, sand, or gravel

- A marking pen

How to Make the Plastic Bottle Bowling Alley

Step 1 Fill the soda bottles half full with dirt, sand, or gravel.

Step 2 Set them up like bowling pins.

Step 3 Number each bottle 1 through 10 with a marking pen.

Step 4 Draw a chalk line on the ground about 12 feet (3.7 meters) in front of the bottles. Players have to stand behind that line when rolling the balls. Adjust chalk line and pins to make the game challenging but not impossible.

How to Play the Plastic Bottle Bowling Alley

Step 1 Players get a running start. Roll the ball and try to knock over pins, like bowling.

Step 2 Players get two rolls.

Step 3 Prizes are awarded by number of points scored.

Garbage Guessing Game:

Here's a guessing game that will raise fun and funds.

You will need these items

- Up to one hundred aluminum cans

- A large box or basket to hold them

- Pencils and scrap paper

- A shoe box or similar box

- Scissors

How to Make the Garbage Guessing Game

Step 1 Count all the cans. Make sure you have the exact number of cans. The object of the game is for players to guess exactly how many cans are in the box. Try not to use an obvious number of cans. For instance, it's a lot easier for someone to guess "one hundred" than "eighty-three."

Step 2 Write down the exact number of cans in the box and give it to an adult for safekeeping.

Step 3 Put all the cans in the box.

Step 4 Cut a slot in the top of the shoe box for players to put their guesses into.

How to Play the Garbage Guessing Game:

Step 1 Players study the number of cans in the box.

Step 2 Players write down the number of cans they think are in the box. They also write their name, address, and phone number. Players put the slip of paper in the shoe box.

Step 3 After the fair is over, sort through the box and find the person who came closest to guessing the number of cans. That person wins a prize. The less people who know the number of cans in the box before the game the better. That way there is less chance of someone giving away the number by accident. (Bottles may also be used).

Hold a Raffle

Have a raffle with one really good prize!

Step 1 Charged a small amount to enter the raffle.

Step 2 Have people fill out their names and phone numbers on scrap paper and put them into a sealed box.

Step 3 At the end of the fair, have a blindfolded person pick one name.

Step 4 Award that person the prize.

A WORD ABOUT PRIZES

People love to win prizes when they go to the fair. Most of your seed money will probably go for prizes to give away to game players. Prizes may be as fancy as your budget or creativity allow. If possible, you may ask store owners to donate prizes for your fair.

Here are some ideas for prizes:

● hand-made crafts

● hand-made art

● small toys

● photographs

● small stuffed animals

● school supplies

● healthy candy or food

● books, posters, and bumperstickers about environmental causes

● tapes, records, CDs

● inexpensive electronics like calculators or tape players

Chapter 6
After the Fair

CLEAN UP TIME!

When the carnival is over, it's time to clean up. Hopefully there won't be too much to do if there are plenty of garbage boxes around. But you want to make sure that you leave the spot where you had the fair cleaner than how you found it. What kind of eco-fair would it be if you leave a big mess? Here are some suggestions:

Step 1
Empty all the glass, aluminum, and recyclable paper and plastic into large boxes or bags. Make sure everything gets recycled.

Step 2
Pick up all the wrappers and trash laying on the ground.

Step 3
Save all the left-over prizes for the next fair or divide them up among the group.

Step 4
Take down the booths and stages. Save what you can for the next eco-fair.

Step 5
Clean everything up so that the area where you had your eco-fair is spotless.

The Final Meeting

After all the booths are taken down and the last bag of trash is hauled away, your group should have a final meeting. Here are some tips:

Step 1 If possible, have a party and a potluck where everybody brings food.

Step 2 Before you start your party, go around the room and ask everybody for their opinion about the fair. What went wrong? What went right? Record your findings in a notebook. Save the notes for your next eco-fair.

Step 3 Read a list of all the money made. Pay back the people who donated the original seed money.

Step 4 Many people will be involved with making your eco-fair a success. You might want to send out thank-you notes to people who donated time, space, and prizes to the fair. Make a list of those people and ask for volunteers to mail the notes.

Step 5 Make arrangements to donate the money to the chosen environmental group.

Step 6 If everyone wants to, make a date for your next eco-fair. You should wait six month to a year before you have another carnival.

Environmental Organizations Who Take Donations:

If you're not sure which of these organizations you want to support, write to them and ask for information about their programs. You may also want to ask how much of your donation actually goes to helping the environment and how much is used for overhead expenses. If you are interested in local environmental groups, look under "Environmental, Conservation, and Ecological Organizations" in the Yellow Pages telephone book. For more information about groups that protect the environment. See the Target Earth™ Earthmobile books *Eco-Groups: Joining Together to Protect the Environment* and *Earth Kids*.

To stop acid rain:
Acid Rain Foundation
1410 Varsity Dr.
Raleigh, N.C. 27606

To save African animals:
African Wildlife Foundation
1717 Massachusetts Ave., N.W.
Washington, D.C. 20036

To save whales:
American Cetacean Society
P.O. Box 2639
San Pedro, California 90731-0943

To insure clean water:
Clean Water Action Project
317 Pennsylvania Ave., S.E.
Washington, D.C. 20003

To save oceans:
The Cousteau Society, Inc.
930 West 21st Street
Norfolk, VA 23517

To protect the environment:
Kids for Saving Earth
P.O. Box 47247
Plymouth, MN 55441

To save the rainforests:
The Rainforest Action Network
301 Broadway
Suite A
San Francisco, CA 94113

To protect wildlife:
World Wildlife Fund
1250 24th Street, N.W.
Washington, D.C. 20037

To save the land, air, & water:
Izaak Walton League of America
1400 Wilson Blvd.
Level B
Arlington, VA 22209

To protect endangered resources:
Natural Resources Defense Council
40 West 20th Street
New York, NY 10011

To save old growth forests:
The Western Canada Wilderness Committee
20 Water Street
Vancouver, B.C. , Canada

For general protection of the environment:
The National Audubon Society
950 Third Avenue
New York, NY 10022

To encourage wise use of the Earth's resources:
The National Wildlife Federation
1400 Sixteenth St. N.W.
Washington, D.C. 20036-2266

To protect rare & endangered species:
The Nature Conservatory
1815 North Lynn Street
Arlington, VA 22209

To stop pesticide pollution & protect oceans:
Rachel Carson Council, Inc.
8940 Mill Rd.
Chevy Chase, MD 20815
San Francisco, CA 94113

To promote conservation of animals & plants:
Sierra Club
730 Polk Street
San Francisco, CA 94109

Connect With Books

Bolton, Reg. *Circus in a Suitcase*. Rowayton, Connecticut: New Plays Incorporated, 1982.

Gryczan, Matthew. *Carnival Secrets*. Royal Oak, Michigan: Zenith Press, 1988.

Schwartz, Linda. *Earthbook For Kids*. Santa Barbara, California: The Learning Works, Inc., 1990.

Thomson, Neil and Ruth. *Fairground Games to Make and Play*. Philadelphia and New York: J.B. Lippincott Company, 1978.

Weedon, Geoff and Ward, Richard. *Fairground Art*. New York: Abbeville Press, 1981.

West, Robin. *Paper Circus*. Minneapolis, Minnesota: Carolrhoda Books, Inc., 1983.

TARGET EARTH™
COMMITMENT

At Target, we're committed to the environment. We show this commitment not only through our own internal efforts but also through the programs we sponsor in the communities where we do business.

Our commitment to children and the environment began when we became the Founding International Sponsor for Kids for Saving Earth, a non-profit environmental organization for kids. We helped launch the program in 1989 and supported its growth to three-quarters of a million club members in just three years.

Our commitment to children's environmental education led to the development of an environmental curriculum called Target Earth,™ aimed at getting kids involved in their education and in their world.

In addition, we worked with Abdo & Daughters Publishing to develop the Target Earth™ Earthmobile, an environmental science library on wheels that can be used in libraries, or rolled from classroom to classroom.

Target believes that the children are our future and the future of our planet. Through education, they will save the world!

TARGET®

Minneapolis-based Target Stores is an upscale discount department store chain of 517 stores in 33 states coast-to-coast, and is the largest division of Dayton Hudson Corporation, one of the nation's leading retailers.